HOW TO STAY IN THE HIGH CALLING

And Not Come Out!

by
Roberts Liardon

Unless otherwise indicated, all Scripture quotations are taken from the *King James Version* of the Bible.

Some quotations are taken from the *New King James Version* of the Bible. Copyright © 1979, 1980, 1982, by Thomas Nelson Inc., publishers.

1st Printing

How To Stay In Your High Calling...And Not Come Out!
ISBN#1-890900-40-0

Copyright © 2000 by Roberts Liardon Ministries
P.O. Box 30710
Laguna Hills, CA 92654-0710

Published by Embassy Publishing Co.
P.O. Box 3500
Laguna Hills, California 92654

Contents

*Chapter
One*

Paul's Midnight Burden

I'd like you to take a moment and imagine the apostle Paul, lying in his prison cell during the final days of his ministry on earth. He's an older man at this point and he's in chains. He's got the scars of being stoned, beaten and left for dead. He has the burden of the churches upon him, relationships which are hard to maintain spiritually. On top of that, his future was not looking very bright because he knew his time to die was approaching.

I'm sure the great apostle Paul had the weight of all those things upon him when, in the middle of the night, he was awakened to pray.

Most would probably assume that Paul would be awakened to pray for one of the baby churches, or even one of the older churches, or maybe one of his fellow apostles. But in the middle of the night, Paul was awakened to pray, not for all those big needs, but for a son in the faith; a son who was not yet carrying great responsibility in the kingdom, but who someday would.

Paul's Burden For His Son

Paul's spirit was opened so the God of Heaven could reach down and touch him in the midnight hour and interrupt the sleep he so desperately needed with a stirring to pray and intercede. God would awaken Paul and say, "Your son Timothy has need of your prayers! If you don't get up and pray, your son may not make it through the trial in which he now stands!"

The trial that was against Timothy was one which every person will face sometime in life. When you're facing negative circumstances and spiritual resistance, God will raise up people to pray for you so you won't draw back from pressing toward the height of what He's asked you to do.

Because of trials and spiritual resistance, many ministers today have repositioned themselves spiritually so it's easier on their soul as well as on those around about them. They're not quitting the ministry, they're just stepping into a lower level of spiritual operation.

This ought not be so! God doesn't want His people to draw back; He wants us to move forward! (Heb 10:39)

Paul was awakened to pray for Timothy, not just so Timothy's faith wouldn't fail, but also so Timothy wouldn't remove himself from his spiritual position. Timothy was stepping back from the post and edge from which he was called to go forward.

Paul's Only Avenue Of Communication

In the day in which Paul lived, there were only two ways he could communicate with a person, face to face or by letter. In the day you and I live, we can pick up our cell phone, or we can send a picture of ourselves over the internet and say hello to somebody on the other side of the world. We can get on a plane and in a matter of hours, we can be in someone's home. Communication today is rapid compared to the time in which Paul lived.

At this point in Paul's life, his chains restricted him from going to Timothy, so the only thing left for him to do was sit down and write him a letter. Paul prayed that as Timothy was reading this letter, it would seem as though Paul himself was standing in front of him speaking.

Paul's Letter To Timothy

Paul starts his letter to Timothy like he did all his letters: *"Paul, an apostle of Jesus Christ by the will of God according to the promise of life which is in Christ Jesus...."* (2 Tim 1:1)

In other words, Paul was saying, "Timothy, I'm an apostle, not by the will of Peter or by the will of the elders at the church of Jerusalem, but by the will of God Almighty. I didn't choose or ask to be an apostle, but I am. I'm a sent one to the earth, and I'm sent for the establishment of the gospel. I'm sent to raise you, my son Timothy, and to make sure you remain at your post.

"Timothy, I live this life of apostleship by this great understanding: I live by the promises that God has given to me. I don't live this life by a promise from some man who never intended to keep it. I cannot live my life on that kind of unsure ground. I live my life and find my security by the promises that God has made to me and you.

"Timothy, I don't go out and speak to the communities and the nations because I have an ego problem or need a platform. I have many things I endure, but I do this because God has promised me life, and He's promised me protection. I walk by faith according to these promises. Remember how I live and walk, Timothy. Remember what I tell you!"

A Divine Relationship

In the 2nd verse of his letter to Timothy, Paul writes, *"To Timothy, my dearly beloved son...."* (2 Tim 1:2) We know by history and Biblical knowledge that there is no biological relationship between Paul and Timothy, not even as an uncle or cousin. Their relationship was divine. It was one that surpassed a blood tie. The Spirit of God tied it together with a holy knot and nothing could break it.

Paul was saying, "Timothy, you're not just my convert, you're someone I have a hope and a heritage in." Paul brings Timothy so close to his heart that he becomes a part of his own being: *"You are my dearly beloved son...."*

Where Are The Apostolic Fathers?

We live in a world today that is looking for apostolic fathers. The next generation of ministers has begun to rise to their pulpits and positions of influence within the kingdom. Some are coming into great power. Behind the door of many of their lives, they are still looking for a Paul to be there for the right purpose. They are looking for a man or a woman, a "mother of Israel," who will stand there with no agenda and say, "I am here for you and you're going to make it! Here is how you walk, here is what you do; you're going to live and obey that high call."

The generation that is rising is not one that is full of arrogance. They are looking for those who are like the apostle Paul. They are looking for those whose hearts are pure, those who have no hidden agendas or desires to use a young man or woman's strength for selfish gain.

Paul said to Timothy, *"You're my dearly beloved son: grace, mercy and peace from God our Father and Jesus His Son, our Lord. I thank God, whom I serve with a pure conscience, as my forefathers did, as without ceasing I remember you in my prayers night and day...."* (2 Tim 1:2-3)

In other words, "Everything I've done, Timothy, I've done because I thought it was right. Even when I was wrong, I thought I was right. When I saw Stephen being stoned, I thought I was doing right. I agreed to it, I said it was a good deed done for God. But now I know I was wrong. And as soon as I found that I was wrong, I turned with the same zeal and began to travel down the route I knew was right. I left my wickedness, Timothy. I repented of my wrongdoing and said, 'with the same strength I did wrong, I now will do right!'"

May God give us those kinds of apostolic men and women today! We need men and women of character who, when they discover a wrong, will turn and not try to hide it or pretend everything is right! Instead, they will say, "I was wrong," and then go with the same zeal down the road that is right!

True Apostolic Fathers Won't Kill Zeal!

Why is it that religion always kills the zeal in the young? Why do we stop the drummer from playing the way he wants to play under the anointing? Why do we stop those kinds of things and try to "mature" them? We're killing the holy zeal of God! Don't kill their zeal, just add knowledge to it! Let the fire keep burning!

Paul was an apostolic father who knew how to help situations and make adjustments without killing young people's zeal. As we raise students and young men and women of the faith, let's not kill the zeal that's in their spirits and in their minds. Let's add knowledge and support and help them run the race God has set before them! ■

Chapter Two

Backing Away From Your High Call

I have a letter I keep next to my bed, written to me from Dr. Lester Sumrall before he passed away. I've received several letters from him over the years, but this letter was different than all the rest. In this letter, Dr. Sumrall wrote, "The last few days I've been praying for you and I want you to know that I believe in you...," then he went on to write about some other things. But that first paragraph showed me a lot about the heart of an apostolic father. Here was a man who was consumed with a vision of feeding the hungry people of the world. He would come to my church and hold up little pictures we could barely see from the platform, and say, "Here's my new boat." Every time he came to my church he had a new project he wanted us to help pay for. I loved it, and our church and ministry was always excited about helping him.

When I received this particular letter I thought, "Here he is, the head of an extensive international ministry, and he took time to pray for me."

That's what Paul was saying to Timothy when he wrote, "...*without ceasing I remember you in my prayers night and day....*" (2 Tim 1:3).

In other words, Paul was saying, "In the middle of the night when I should be sleeping, I'm awakened to pray for you, Timothy. I'm awakened to assist you by the means of prayer so you will not fail or move from your spiritual post. I want you to know that you're not just a name on a list that I appeal to for money, you're not just another person I'm covering, *you're a beloved son.* In the middle of the night, when I should be praying for the church at Jerusalem, and the other one I'm planting across town, I'm awakened and my spirit is disturbed over you. I want you to know that you're not out there alone. God is showing me what you're up to. You may think you're alone, and you may feel like you've been cut-off and that I'm thousand miles away, but I still know where you're at and how you're doing. I've been awakened in the middle of the night. I know the night terrors you've been facing; I know the night dreams that have come to haunt you! I've had them in my life too. I want you to know that I long to see you my son, but I'm restrained. If I could, I would shake the chains from me right now and I'd be on my way to your home. I'd get there as fast as I could because my heart and my soul longs to be with you!

"Timothy, I know your state. I know that you've been disturbed and that the temptation to withdraw is all around you. I understand where you're at and I know how to get you back into the joy of your call."

Timothy's Dire State

Timothy was in his home, facing the pressure of a young, large church which was being severely persecuted. Timothy was probably one of the Christians the persecutors were looking to kill. I'm sure they figured that if they killed the leader, they'd scare the people away. Timothy was also facing the pressure of finding homes for the orphans whose parents were martyred in the theaters of Rome a few days before. The church members would take care of the young babies, some six months old, some eight years old and some twelve. Timothy had to do his best to find families who would care for the siblings together and not split them up.

He also had to be concerned that the order and atmosphere of his church stayed right. He had to be sure that he preached messages on the right things so everybody was being touched. On top of that, he had to maintain a life he could call his own. All this pressure, as well as the prince of the territory, probably raged at this man. Timothy had a willing heart; he didn't recoil from his duty or say "No" to responsibility. Nevertheless, the pressure had begun to mount, and it was beginning to take its toll upon his life.

Timothy Was Losing His Edge

Timothy wasn't quitting his ministry, he was simply moving from his post and from the edge of the Spirit where he belonged. You see, you can continue preaching but be in the wrong position, spiritually. Many church leaders in the nations love Jesus with all of their heart, but they have not learned how to remain at their post during times of pressure. Paul was not just trying to save Timothy from quitting ministry, Paul was trying to keep him in his high call and on the cutting edge of the will of God. ∎

Chapter Three

Timothy's Heritage Of Faith

*A*fter assuring Timothy that he was praying for him, the apostle Paul changes his tone for a moment. He says, *"Timothy I want to remind you of something."* (2 Tim 1:5)

Why would someone have to be reminded of something? Because they have forgotten it! Some things are forgotten in degrees, while other things are lost completely until you are reminded of them. You probably didn't even know you had forgotten them! Refreshing lost or forgotten truth is an apostolic function.

Paul said, *"Timothy, I want to remind you of where you came from."* (2 Tim 1:5)

The first thing Paul did to put Timothy back where he belonged was remind him of the heritage of his faith. He said, "Timothy, I remind you of what kind of faith you came from. When I held my first crusade in the city where your mother and your grandmother lived, you were there. After the crusade was over, your grandmother invited me to your home. Your mother had gone early to prepare a meal for me, and the neighbors next door left because they found out I was coming and thought there might be a riot.

"I remember that as I sat down in the chair, I looked down the little hallway of your home, and you came walking down the hall. You sat down in front of me and just looked. You didn't ask any questions, you just stared at the scar on my face and the bandages on my hand that were covering the injury I received during my meeting. You heard me talk about the things that God had done for me, and where I was going next. And then your mother and your grandmother begged me to pray for you before I left.

"I came back another time and the same thing occurred. Your mother and your grandmother have a degree of faith that is not found in many hearts. There are some people who have sweet faith, just enough to get to heaven with, but they go through hell while they're here on earth. They love sweet Jesus, but they won't do anything for Him. There are others who have a little more grit to their faith, but just enough to be faithful to attend a church. They would never go to the unreached regions of the earth to preach, they barely give ten percent of their income! In fact, the thought of giving more has probably never even crossed their mind!

"But you didn't come from that kind of stock, Timothy. Your faith is different than that! I've never had to worry about the temperament of your faith; you've got the grit that came from your mother and your grandmother. Inside your spirit is a degree of faith that has propelled you to the place you're in right now. It moved inside as I spoke and trained you. The temperament of your faith caused you to grow quicker than others.

"In the light of all this, my son Timothy, why is it that now in the time that you call a crisis, your faith seems to be dormant? Why is it that now, when you're gritty faith should be at its height, it is silent and nearly gone?

"I remind you of where your faith came from and what kind of faith it is! And I'm persuaded it's still in you! *Get up Timothy!* Get your faith moving again! If the devil can stop your faith, he can stop you from hearing, seeing, receiving and obeying!"

My Personal Heritage Of Faith

I come from the same type of spiritual heritage as Timothy. Inside my spirit dwells a degree of faith that I did not receive from my father. I got it from two gritty women — my grandmother and my mother! I know that sounds strange, but that's the best way I know how to say it! My grandmother and my mother are real nice, but they've got some spiritual grit to them!

When my father left my mother with nothing but a dime to her name, she didn't cry and go on welfare! She didn't run around looking for self-pity from everyone! She pulled herself up and brought me and my sister through that crisis and put us where we are today. That's called grit!

I want to remind some of you who are reading this book that you also have come from that kind of faith!

"But Pastor Roberts, I'm the first Christian in my family line!"

Okay, maybe you don't have a natural heritage of faith to draw from like I did, but you can start one! You have the faith to do it! You can start a new line of faith by showing your family the kind of grit that is required to go through anything! Your family needs someone with grit and audacity to show them how to do things right! *You've got to do it — no one else will!*

I'm persuaded that this kind of faith is in you, dear reader! You can't tell me that it's not there! Inside your belly lives *the roar* of faith! What has dominated your life until now has been the heaviness of your soul and the weariness of your physical man. But inside your belly, where the rivers of living water flow and never run dry, there is faith that needs to be released. Get up and get that faith moving again! ■

Chapter

Four

Valuing The Gift Of God

*I*n his letter to Timothy, Paul went on to say, "I also want to remind you of something else you seem to have forgotten, my son. I remind you that inside of your spirit resides a gift from God. Not everybody has the kind of gift you've got; some would give everything they own just to have half of what you carry." (2 Tim 1:6)

Did you know there are people in world who would pay the ultimate price for what some carry so carelessly? I've seen this many times in my journeys. I don't understand how people can look upon their spiritual gifts so carelessly. They take it for granted that out of the billions of people in the world, God chose them to carry such a tremendous responsibility. I don't understand how someone can live such a careless life and only look at things from a temporal viewpoint.

One of the great keys of living a full life is seeing everything the way Heaven sees it. It changes the way you view things. There is danger when you allow a temporal mindset to become the glasses through which you look at the world. It is dangerous to live by the voice of carnality. There's a sound that comes from Heaven which you must never let out of your ears. You must never live a day without acknowledging God's divine presence within your human spirit. That's exactly what Paul was trying to get Timothy to understand. He was saying, "Timothy, inside your belly there's a gift. It's not an earthly or intellectual gift; it's a heavenly treasure hidden away deep inside your earthen vessel. Don't try to tell me you don't have it, and don't try to tell me that it was just the temporary touch of an anointing! I know a spiritual gift is in you because God used my hands to place it there! Remember that afternoon, during that meeting not too many years ago, when the Spirit of God fell upon us? Remember it, Timothy? Remember how, by the leading of the Spirit of God, Jesus sent me to you? Suddenly, in my hands there was a power I've only known at certain times in my life. Remember how God directed me to lay my hands upon you? I laid my hands upon you and people began to cry. A holy presence filled the room.

Not everyone understood what was taking place, but they all felt the atmosphere change! It was not a casual event, Timothy, it was something that the throne room of Heaven had ordered to take place. Out of my spirit and through my hands came a portion of the gift God has given me; and it went into you. That is why when you get up to preach and teach, people say, 'He speaks and acts like Paul!' Don't ever be worried about that because you carry a part of my DNA, my makeup, my spiritual chromosomes. God took a part of what He put in me and put it inside of you! You'll never be able to tell me the gift is not there! You'll never be able to say that the time and season of your anointing has ended! I know what you carry, Timothy, because it also resides in me! Get off your rear-end and stir it back up!

"Timothy, a gift not stirred makes the inside sad! But a gift that is stirred gives life and light to everyone around! Let your faith rise again and stir your gift! Let it come back to the place where it belongs! You'll only find joy when your gift is functioning at maximum power!

"Timothy, when my gift is at maximum power, they try to kill me, they try to stone me and they want to do all kinds of evil things to me; but my highest ecstasy in God comes when I'm in the midst of a riot! I'm in my highest place of joy when they're trying to hunt me down to kill me!

"I know it sounds strange, but this gift in you will bring that kind of mentality. I know it's in you, Timothy! Don't try to get rid of it or you'll start malfunctioning as a man of God."

Paul's Fatherly Advice

Paul was trying to get Timothy to understand the nature of the apostolic gift which had been imparted to him. Paul understood the seriousness of Timothy's situation and gave Timothy the fatherly advice he needed to stir his gift and step into the height of his call. ■

Chapter Five

Don't Be Overwhelmed By Fear

G *od has not given us a spirit of fear, Timothy,"* Paul continued, *"but of power and of love and of a sound mind...."* (2 Tim 1:7)

"Timothy, God never uses fear as a teacher! When you wake up in the middle of the night and fear has entered your bedroom, you don't have to put up with its presence! When you go out to pastor your church or hold an outreach meeting in your city and you hear that those who hate you are coming to take you to prison and kill you, don't fear! Sometimes fear will live in a three-foot radius around you, but fear has not been sent by God! If it wasn't for the glory of the Lord, that fear would have already overwhelmed you! If it wasn't for the angels that surround you, that fear would have already fallen upon you! You can feel it sometimes, only a few feet away, screaming at you!

"I want you to know that I've felt that same spirit. I've had to deal with the spirit of fear a lot, but I know this to be a truth: God has never given any man the spirit of fear! He doesn't send fear to teach you a lesson! He doesn't use fear as a taskmaster or a school teacher! Timothy, God doesn't test men with fear!

"Whenever you feel fear closing in, deal with it as your arch enemy! Attack it with everything you've got and destroy its voice and presence in your life! I know what fear is like, and I've conquered it! That's why they call me bold, Timothy! That's why some run from me. That's why some try to undermine my words behind my back! They're too chicken to come before my face! That's why they lie and tell half-truths about me!

"I know what it's like to deal with fear, Timothy. I know what you're facing now, but God has given us three things to overcome fear with: power, love and a sound mind! I remind you that when you feel weak, there is power inside of you! When you feel helpless, the Holy Ghost will energize you and lift you into a place you've not known. Power unlimited abides in you, and it's available to you whenever you need it!

"Timothy, when you feel the pain of those hateful words that come at you, He has given you great love to help you overcome. In the midst of the storm, He will give you a soundness and a stability that you won't find in any counselor's office or in any medication. He will give you soundness of mind so you can sleep at night."

Are You Ashamed Of The Gospel?

"Timothy, you are withdrawing from preaching the gospel the right way! Don't be ashamed of the testimony of our Lord Jesus."

Why would Paul have to tell Timothy not to be ashamed of the Lord? If I asked you if you were ashamed of the gospel, you would probably say, "No way!" If I asked certain pastors that same question today, they'd probably say the same thing. Yet, many around the world are no longer preaching the gospel with strength and boldness because of shame. Some will preach salvation, but they won't preach deliverance. Some will preach healing, but they won't preach prosperity. Some will preach the resurrection and the cross, but they won't preach other things. The parts of the Bible they won't preach, they camouflage with religious statements like, "That's not my calling." The truth is: *they're ashamed of that part of the gospel!*

Timothy was not withdrawing from preaching, he was drawing back from *the way* he was preaching! He was withdrawing from the *height* of his call!

You can keep preaching the same things over and over but lose the "punch" of faith and the grit to believe what you are preaching. The great evangelist, T. L. Osborn, says it this way: "There is power in the announcement of the gospel." In other words, there is power in the way the gospel is spoken. There is power in the way it is presented to the heart of people.

The apostle Paul was saying, "Timothy, you're not announcing the gospel right because you're ashamed! You're preaching it, but the joy of it is not there. The *fight of faith* is not there! (1 Tim 6:12) You're preaching the gospel from a withdrawn, safe posture! I didn't train you like that! I have never lived or preached that way at any time in my life! There's no joy when you live like that, Timothy!

"I'm one of the greatest enemies of religion because I'll never stop preaching the gospel the way God gave it to me! I'll never withdraw from my announcement, my body language, my tone or my spiritual posture! I'll say it the same way as I get older, and I'll say it better! Timothy, I command you to get up and get back to doing what you have learned from me! If you're truly my son, return to your post of correct announcement! I've not labored in prayer for you and given you my time just to *hope* you would make it! I gave these things to you because *you're going to make it!* I'm your father in the faith! The DNA that runs in your spiritual veins not only comes from God, but from me as well! Timothy, how dare you stand there and say your gift has changed! How dare you bow to the kiss-butt religiosity I've been fighting my entire life! Get back into the fight of faith! Keep pressing toward the mark of your high call in Christ Jesus and stand with me for the defense of the gospel!" ■

Chapter Six

Don't Be Ashamed Of My Chains

"Timothy, let me remind you of another thing while we're at it. Let me remind you of these chains I have on my hands that rattle while I write this letter. Don't be ashamed of me, His prisoner."

2 Tim 1:8

imothy was withdrawing from his father in the faith because it wasn't "politically correct" for Timothy to be that close to Paul. The men from Timothy's denomination had come by and said, "Timothy,

33

we see promise in you. Out of all the young pastors and preachers, we think you're the best. We feel like we're supposed to get behind you and make things happen for you. But there are some issues we need to discuss with you and that's why we've come. The issue that concerns us most is your relationship with Paul. Paul is a unique man, we all admit that, but we don't understand him. We respect him from a distance. We've been in your meetings, Timothy. We've sent our spies to see how you've been doing. You have sound doctrine, wholesome character, a good flow in the gifts of the Spirit, a good anointing; the only problem is, *you act like Paul too much!* You refer to him too often, and your mannerisms are too much like his. If you could adjust all that, we could get behind you. We aren't saying don't be his friend. We're just asking you to keep it private so the babes in Christ won't be confused.

"You know, Timothy, if you follow Paul too closely — you'll be just like him: *a jail bird.* He knows more about jails than anybody in our whole ministerial realm. He knows which jail has the best bread and which one has the worst; he knows them all! Do you want to be known as the jail bird, Timothy? If you follow Paul too closely, that's what will happen to you."

Watch Out For Man's Temporal Viewpoint

These men saw Paul in the wrong light. They viewed him from a temporal religious viewpoint and they didn't see that he was a mighty apostle of the Most High God! They also didn't understand that God had arranged a divine relationship between Timothy and Paul. The anointing that rested so mightily upon Paul was beginning to rest upon Timothy through apostolic succession. This eternal gift and apostolic deposit was to live on in the earth through Paul's young successor. That's why Paul said, "Timothy, don't be ashamed of me, His prisoner. I didn't ask for this apostolic responsibility. You've heard me tell the story many times. I was on the road to Damascus, looking for Christians to bind and throw in jail, when suddenly a light came from heaven and knocked me and my assistants to the ground! My assistants only heard a voice, but I saw a man! His name was Jesus and He said *'I have need of you.'*

"I found that I was wrong to persecute the Christians, and I repented of what I had been doing that same afternoon. Before that day, I was sure I was doing the right thing. My religious education said I was right, and my peers did too! In fact, my colleagues praised me for my zeal! But that afternoon on the Damascus Road, something happened to me that not only changed my life, but also the life of the Church! This anointing that works through my mouth and moves me the way it does also provokes the crowd. It's not an ability to play-act and draw people's attention — it's a gift from God that bears great lasting fruit. It's a gift from God that enables me to endure the harassment, the affliction, the resistance and the persecution. You carry this same gift, Timothy! Don't withdraw from me and don't think I'm this way by choice — *although I willingly obey.* But I'm telling you my son, this powerful apostolic grace rests upon you too! Stop trying to run from it! It may not be developed as strongly as it is in me yet, but it will grow. It's going to have a voice! So, you better learn now how to stand by your true friend and know who is family and who is not! I'm telling you, these people who are talking to you have flattering lips — they're *not* your friends! Those who are promising the sky can't give you a bucket of dirt! Don't be ashamed of me, His prisoner!

"Timothy, be a participant in the afflictions of the gospel according to the power of God that you walk in (2 Tim 1:8). Quit thinking it's strange that every time you get a new anointing, a new type of demon shows up to resist you. It all goes together; you can't have one without the response of the other. The devil is not going to let you walk through with a strong apostolic call on your life and just say, 'Who cares, no threats, no worry, everything is fine!' The devil may have some dumb followers, but he is not stupid! He can see things spiritually and he'll wait and watch. He'll wait for the right moment to execute his conspiracy! Timothy, know it now, principalities and powers strategize and attack high-level gifts and calls!"

Conclusion

So there we have it; we see how an apostolic father relates to a son in the faith: "Paul, an apostle of Jesus Christ by the will of God, living my life according to the promises that are in Christ Jesus. I write to you Timothy, my dearly beloved son in the faith. Grace, mercy and peace be unto you from God our Father and our Lord Jesus Christ. Timothy, I've always served the God of my forefathers with a pure conscience. I know what you're going through Timothy, and I want you to know that I've been praying for you night and day. You're not there alone; somebody is standing in the gap for you!

"I long to be with you! You're special to me; you're close, you're dear and you're my son! Timothy, I can't come to you right now, so I have written this letter instead. I hope the runner gets there on time! I know what's going on in your life; maybe not the details, but I know enough about what you're going through to tell you that my joy is affected too!

"Let me remind you of a truth that young men forget when they're under the attack of the enemy. Let me remind you where your faith came from. Your mother and grandmother's faith is known throughout all of Asia, and I speak of it often. I encourage other women in their faith by telling them about your mother and grandmother. I am persuaded that their faith is in you too! So activate it and get it working again!

"I know the devil has tried to shut your gift down and make you think it's not there. Stir it up, my son because it's always there! God's gifts come without repentance, and you can't get rid of them (Rom 11:29). You can go to the wildest parts of the world and try to forget God, but He's there, and your gift is still living inside your spirit! And don't try to tell me you don't have it, Timothy, because God used my hands to place it in you! That's why people think you're putting on a show and acting like me!

"Timothy, don't be ashamed to follow me! Don't ever be ashamed of your spiritual DNA and how God put you together! Fear is never a teacher, either! God will give you love, power, and a sound mind in the midst of your storm! Timothy, be a man of God, and get your butt back out there where it belongs! Preach the full gospel, and preach it the right way! Announce it with joy unspeakable! Let God's temperament come on your face and shine! Let the glory come out of you when you step up to preach! Preach like a man from another world! That's the way God has called you, and that's the way I've trained you! Return to your post, and don't listen to the flattering lips of religious men! Timothy, I'm your spiritual father by God's choice, and I am willing to be it! So carry my DNA without shame and get back where you belong, doing the bidding of the Lord!"

That is how Paul put his spiritual son back where he belonged, in the high call of his place in ministry. ■

Spirit Life Partner

Roberts Liardon

Wouldn't It Be Great...

- If you could feed over 1,000 hungry people every week?
- If you could travel 250,000 air miles, boldly preaching the Word of God in 94 nations?
- If you could strengthen and train the next generation of God's leaders?
- If you could translate 31 books and distribute them into 47 languages?

...Now You Can!

Maybe you can't go, but by supporting this ministry every month, your gift can help to communicate the gospel around the world.

SLBC graduates ministering in the Philippines—provided by Spirit Life Partners world-wide. Thank you for your ongoing support!

------------------ ✂ CLIP ALONG LINE & MAIL TO ROBERTS LIARDON MINISTRIES. ------------------

☐ **YES!!** Pastor Roberts, I want to support your work in the kingdom of God by becoming a **SPIRIT LIFE PARTNER.** Please find enclosed my first monthly gift.

Name_____

Address_____

City_____ State _____ Zip _____

Phone ( )_____ Email_____

SPIRIT LIFE PARTNER AMOUNT: $_____

☐ Check / Money Order   ☐ VISA   ☐ American Express   ☐ Discover   ☐ MasterCard

☐☐☐☐☐ ☐☐☐☐☐ ☐☐☐☐☐ ☐☐☐☐☐

Name On Card_____ Exp. Date___/___/___

Signature_____ Date ___/___/___

Roberts Liardon Ministries

P.O. Box 30710 ♦ Laguna Hills, CA 92654 USA ♦ (949) 833-3555 ♦ Fax (949) 833.9555 ♦ www.robertsliardon.org

ꓤOOKS
by Roberts Liardon

A Call to Action
Accessing Your Hidden Greatness
Almost Christian: Exposing the Two-Faced Believer
Breaking Controlling Powers:
(A Compilation of 3 Bestselling Books)
Cry of the Spirit
Don't Let the Devil Destroy Your Purpose
Extremists, Radicals and Non-Conformists
Final Approach
Forget Not His Benefits
God's Generals
Greater, Wiser, Stronger: God Wants You To Increase!
Haunted Houses, Ghosts and Demons
How to Get Your Spirit in Shape and Keep It
How to Stay in Your High Calling and Not Come Out!
I Saw Heaven
Kathryn Kuhlman
Knowing People by the Spirit
On Her Knees
Religious Politics
School of the Spirit
Sharpening Your Discernment
Smith Wigglesworth - Complete Collection
Smith Wigglesworth Speaks to Students
The Most Dangerous Place to Be
The Spirit of Reformation: You Can Change The World
3rd Degree Burn: How You Can Burn Hotter for God!
Three Outs and You're In
Why The Devil Doesn't Want You to Pray in Tongues
You Can Jumpstart Your Gift

Roberts Liardon Ministries
International Offices

USA	**EUROPE**	**SOUTH AFRICA**	**PHILIPPINES**
P.O. Box 30710	Roberts Liardon Ministries	Roberts Liardon Ministries	Roberts Liardon Ministries
Laguna Hills, CA 92654-0710	P.O. Box 295	P.O. Box 3155	P.O. Box 154
Phone (949) 833.3555	Welwyn Garden City	Kimberly 8300	IloIlo City 5000
Fax (949) 833.9555	AL7 2ZG England	South Africa	(6333) 329.4537
Website: www.robertsliardon.org	011-44-1707-327-222	011-27-53-832-1207	Email: rlm-phil@iloilo.net

---

Spirit Life Bible College
"Preparation is never lost time" — Roberts Liardon
Call today for more information: (949) 833.3555